grown-up shmown-up

rediscover your inner child

by nicky allen

a grown-up shmown-up book

ISBN: 978-0-692-89329-6

Library of Congress Cataloging-in-Publication Data

Allen, Nicky

grown-up shmown-up / by Nicky Allen

some people think at a certain age you have to become a grown-up.

i say grown-up shmown-up. growing up is a trap. it's a sham, don't buy into it. it sucks.

once you buy into it and start becoming a "grown-up", you start losing your spark, your originality, your imagination, and your creativity. your fire dims.

if you have grown up, or starting to grow up, and it sucks, then you need to rediscover your inner child.

your mission...

finish this entire journal.

this is _____ _____'s
anti-grown-up journal.

- i will keep this journal with me at all times.

- things will get messy, funny, childish, and annoying (to my friends & family), but i will persevere.

because i _____ being a grown-up.

and i want to start _____.

what you'll need:

yo

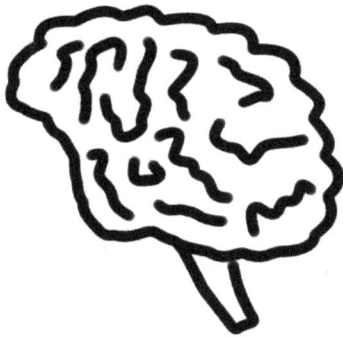

im

ur

ag

in

at

ion

Look in the mirror and
draw yourself.

this is me before grown-up
shmown-up.

take a selfie with this
journal, upload on social
media, use hashtag
#grownupshmownup

flip the journal
upside down.

flip your world upside down.

who was your hero
when you were little?

draw your hero here.

flip back around.

what would you say to someone if you could get away with it?

(write it here, then mark it out)

[redacted]

color this in. don't stay
inside the lines.

what was your favorite
song when you were
little?

listen to it!

how did you feel?

List 5 things that really make you smile:

1.

2.

3.

4.

5.

If you could be a
superhero, what would
be your power & your
name?

draw you as a superhero.

make a cape out of a
sheet, and announce
your superhero name &
power to everyone.

now draw your super
villain.
mwa-ha-ha-ha

then destroy him.

if you could go to any
planet, which one would
you visit?

draw you standing on it.

create a cartoon
character.

what's the character's
name & catch phrase?

what did you used to
enjoy but haven't done
since you were a kid?

now do it.

how did you feel?

have each of your
friends draw you on
these pages.

now draw your friends
who drew you on the
previous pages.

rub the Lamp. now
write your 3 wishes.

1.

2.

3.

wonder

make believe

make a paper airplane
out of this page.

$\longrightarrow$

try to make it as
aerodynamic as possible.

what's your longest fly
time?

put on your favorite
song, and dance like
nobody is looking, even
if they are.

write what you think
Life is Like 3000 years
from now.

write what you think
Life is Like 3000 years
ago.

right now, what do you

see:

smell:

hear:

taste:

feel:

what was your favorite cartoon when you were little?

watch it!

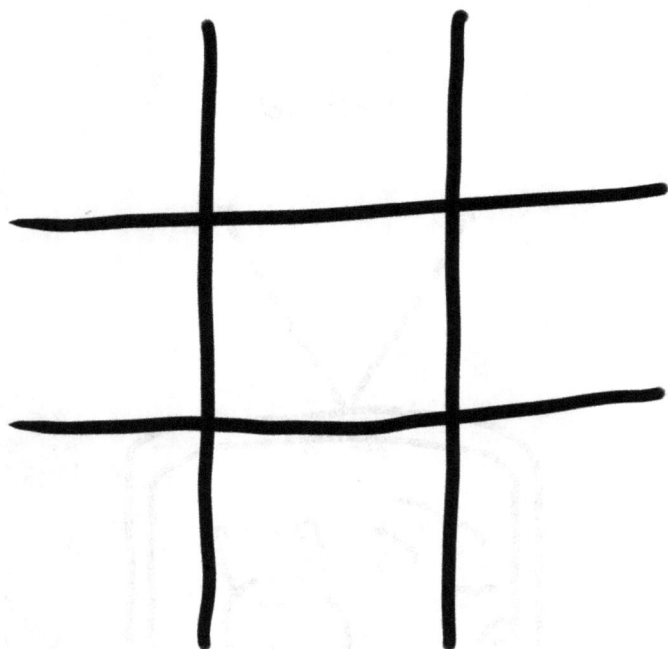

play tic-tac-toe with someone.

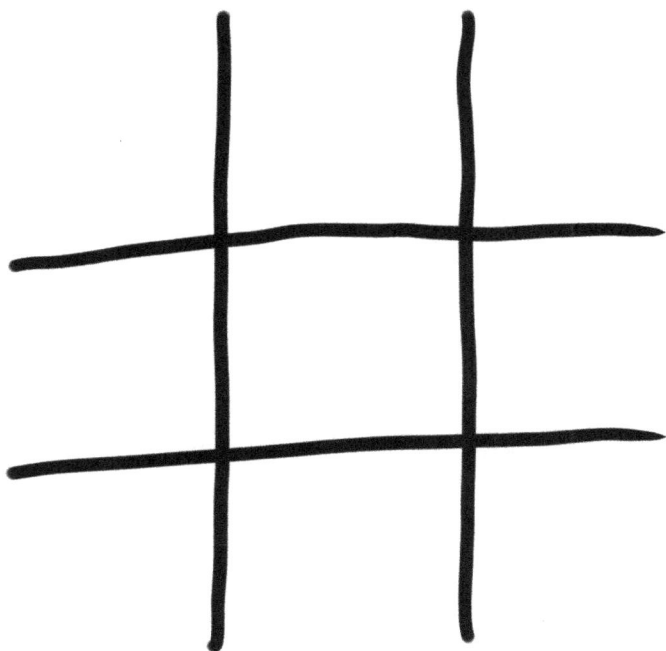

get all of your friends
to sign these pages.

co-write an adventure
story with your best
friend, about you two.

(take the following pages)

bff adventure story

bff adventure story cont...

2

bff adventure story cont...

inside my
pockets/purse
right now:

(tape some things
here)

if i were invisible i
would:

go to:

see:

take:

push:

sneak in:

watch:

play pranks on:

hit:

lol

go annoy someone for 1 minute. Longer if it's really funny.

dear past me,

dear future me,

play a game with
someone and
cheat at it.

did they catch you?

find some pictures of
you when you were a kid.

tape them here, and write what
you loved about that time.

$\longrightarrow$

build a fort.

invite someone in.

fingerpaint anything on
these pages.

what would you do if you won the lottery?

go to:

buy:

give money to:

and:

if you could switch
Lives with someone, who
would it be?

why?

now List reasons why
that person would want
to switch lives with you!

reasons:

if your personality was a color, what would it be?

draw your personality then color it with your color.

dress in something fun today. if you can't, then wear it when you get home.

what did you wear?

how did you feel?

how did others react?

play time.

play something you
Loved when you were a
kid. try to get someone
to play with you.

what did you play?

who played with you?

write the first page of a novel about YOU!

I

who is your best friend?

why?

now have them write
why you're their best
friend.

play hide-n-seek with
someone.

draw a monster you are
scared of.

now destroy him!

make a list of 5 things
you didn't say because
you were scared.

1.

2.

3.

4.

5.

List 3 people you couldn't live without:

1.

2.

3.

show them this page.

List 5 places you want to visit:

1.

2.

3.

4.

5.

startle someone.

tehe

what happened?

Write your name, the date, your phone number, and your address with your feet!

with your left hand,
write how you feel
today and what
happened.

if you were a famous
singer, what would your
stage name be?

why?

what would be your
first song title?

connect the dots.

then color in and add toppings
you love.

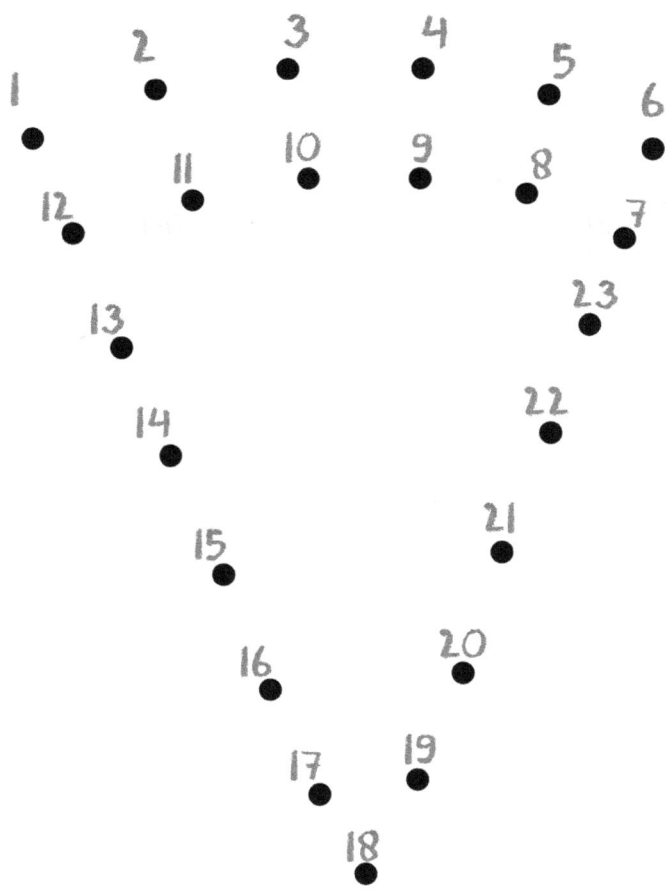

who has hurt you
recently?

try to tell them why you were
hurt.

the grown-up thing is usually to hold it in. channel your inner child and let it out.

how did it go?

daydream about your
fantasy life.

write everything you daydreamed
about:

find & paste a picture of
your dream car here.

cloud gaze for a while.
List things & animals
that you see in the
clouds.

draw them on these pages.
(if there are no clouds today, save this
page for another day)

save this page for the next time it rains.

sing and dance in the rain.

List 5 things you would change about the world:

1.

2.

3.

4.

5.

make up a cool half
song & sing it!

verse:

chorus:

$\left(\overline{\text{insert prompt here}} \right)$

do something kind

if you were stranded on a deserted island, what 5 things & 1 person would you bring?

what things?

1.

2.

3.

4.

5.

what person?

1.

if you could talk to
any animal, what animal
would it be?

why?

what was your last
dream about?

what do you think it means?

don't take yourself
too seriously!

do something you think
is fun.

what did you do?

$\left(\overline{\text{insert prompt here}} \right)$

do something hilarious
(far beyond funny. must be HILARIOUS)

you know what to do.

if you were 5 again,
what do you want to be
when you grow up?

things i will start
doing to keep from
growing up again:

1.

2.

3.

4.

5.

6.

7.

8.

9.

10.

Look in the mirror and
draw yourself.

this is me after grown-up
shmown-up.

~~the end~~
the beginning

for more information,
and more from nicky
allen visit
grownupshmownup.com

never grow up